LONDON MEMORIES

Compiled by Russell Fell
Images David G Savage

CW00953041

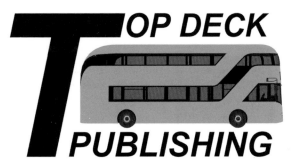

TOP DECK PUBLISHING

© Design: Transport Treasury 2024. Text: Russell Fell
ISBN 978-1-913893-43-9

First published in 2024 by Transport Treasury Publishing Limited. 16 Highworth Close,
High Wycombe, HP13 7PJ

Top Deck Publishing is an imprint of Transport Treasury Publishing.

www.ttpublishing.co.uk

Printed by Short Run Press Ltd., Exeter.

Front cover: Edmonton's K3 1681 pulls away fron the stop in front of Shoreditch Church. Not far to go now before it reaches its Liverpool Street destination. Despite being a Sunday, there are plenty of people around and the bus looks to be quite full. That's because of the various traditional Sunday markets in this area. The three K classes were a complete Leyland vehicle. The K3 sub-class followed the earlier two a couple of years later towards the end of 1940. The one distinguishing factor of the K3s was that the sidelights were built into the front panels instead of projecting from the sides. The K3s were always associated with Edmonton depot. The bus behind is RT4608 on the 35A, which was a summer Sundays only route that, instead of running to Chingford Hatch, ran to Chingford, Royal Forest Hotel on the edge of Epping Forest. DGS34-3

Rear cover: RT2282 has just begun its journey on the 145 from the Dagenham Kent Avenue terminus on New Road to the Royal Forest Hotel at Chingford. It's turning left out of Heathway into Hedgemans Road by the Church Elm pub. RT2282 was a Barking vehicle at the time. On a Sunday the route had an allocation of 8RTs in June 1962, with three from Barking and five from Upton Park. What I like about this picture are the two elm trees that flank the bus. Hedgemans Road would have been on the southern perimeter of the vast Becontree Housing Estate. Behind the bus to the left and just along Heathway would have been Dagenham Heathway station. On the side of the bus is an advert for Oliver! , the stage-musical with music and lyrics by Lionel Bart. Opening in June 1960 at the New Theatre in London, it ran for three highly successful years before moving on t Broadway in 1963.

David Savage Collection 1960-63
Introduction

It is a great pleasure to introduce this album of bus photos from the David Savage archive. For David photographing buses and coaches was to become a lifetime's hobby. From an early age David developed an interest in London's buses, just as I did. His home was in Dagenham on the Becontree Housing Estate, living at 104 Hunters Hall Road. His interest was, if not inspired by, then at least probably aided by one of Ian Allan ABCs of London Buses. Growing up in the 1950s train spotting was a popular hobby among boys, and it was mainly boys, all over the country, fascinated by steam locomotives. For those of us growing up in London we had an added option and that was collecting bus numbers. The Ian Allan ABCs played a big part in encouraging and nurturing these hobbies.

After he left Robert Clack Comprehensive School in 1959, David went to work at Wains engineering firm before switching a year later to Ilford Limited, a famous company producing film for cameras, film paper and chemicals for developing and fixing films. The company was founded in 1879 by Alfred Hugh Harman as the Britannia Works, initially producing photography plates. In 1902 he changed its name to Ilford Limited, for Ilford was where it had its works. A year later the company set up a factory at Brentwood in Woodman Road, and this later was known locally as "Selo Works".

Working for Ilford enabled David to acquire film at reduced rates, which was important in those days for film was not cheap. David's first bus photos were in 1960 when he was sixteen. To begin with these were taken locally at Barking, Becontree Heath and West Ham, focusing on what was new and what was soon to disappear like the pre-war RTs, employed as trainers in their retirement. He realized that trolleybuses were being phased out and these he set out to photograph before it was too late. Like me he preferred to go on his photographic expeditions alone. Using Rover tickets, we were able to travel all over London and beyond relatively cheaply. When he was 18, he bought his first car, a mini, and this enabled him to explore the country area of London Transport more conveniently.

It's easy to forget now how different photography was in those days. Film materials were not cheap, and cameras were limited in their abilities. In particular only the more expensive cameras had the range of speeds needed to capture moving vehicles in sharp focus. Photographers also had to use light meters to select the correct diaphragm opening (the f number) to match the chosen speed, and focusing had to be done manually. Like many amateur photographers David had to rely initially on second hand cameras like Rolleicord, Rolleiflex and Bronica, which were medium-format roll film cameras, and in their day, they were highly regarded. Throughout much of his photographic career, he worked with both 35mm SLF and the medium format roll film cameras, and normally he would take both types of camara with him. Eventually he moved on to Canons. The Canon A1 in particular was a superb camera. Although he moved on to slides and colour film, David never ventured into digital. His preference, though, was always for black and white, which he developed and printed himself.

Unlike David, my interest in trains and buses had rather tailed off by 1960. What rekindled it was coming to work in High Wycombe in 1970 and seeing green RTs and RFs again, which brought back so many memories. Passing the school where I was teaching were RTs and RMLs on the 326 (Micklefield to Sands, Mill End Road), RFs on the local 442 serving new Hicks Farm Estate and Hatters Lane, RMLs from Windsor and Staines garages on the 441 (Staines, Windsor to High Wycombe), and finally there was the unreliable RC class on the Green Line 711 (Reigate – High Wycombe).

Before I started photographing buses myself in 1973, I had begun collecting bus photos, partly in the hope of finding a photograph of my father while driving an RT on his regular M-F 4/4A routes. At the weekend he would work on the other Holloway (J) routes. Before the RTs he drove STs and STLs, and strangely enough perhaps, he always maintained the latter were more comfortable to drive than the RTs. Unfortunately, that search for a photo of my father ultimately proved elusive. My father had died in 1969, and when I heard his old garage was about to close, I went back there for one last visit. This was in September 1971, days before its closure. I wanted to remember him there in his heyday and just to bring back those childhood memories of occasionally accompanying him there to pick up his pay. He would take me round the garage. I remember him telling me that originally it had been a horse bus garage. Had it been a tram or trolleybus depot like nearby Highgate, it would no doubt have been more symmetrical. But, in the end, its very lack of symmetry was probably what gave it its character. As as a child I was fascinated by its atmosphere.

When I started buying bus photographs in the early 1970s, there was never any shortage of post war and 1950s images, thanks in large part to photographers like Alan B. Cross. Neither was there any shortage of current ones. What I found lacking were images from the 1960s, and in particular the first half of that decade. So I hope these photos of David's will help to fill this gap.

Most of the photos in this album were taken on a Sunday, because working full-time he would only the have had the weekends free, and back then most of us would only have had two weeks' paid holiday a year. These photos remind us, though, how different Sundays used to be before the 1994 Sunday Trading Act, how quiet the streets of our towns and cities were. This act, by permitting smaller shops to open all day on Sundays, if they wished, and larger ones to open for six hours, was enough to completely transform the character of a typical English Sunday. Mrs. Thatcher had tried to do something similar eight years before, but the bill then had failed to get through Parliament. In 1960 many people still worked Saturday mornings, which in effect would have left only Sundays free for photographic trips across London. Incidentally, the first changes to the working week came from pressure from the workers in factories in the industrial north. This began in the early 19th century, and it led to an increasing number of factory owners allowing the workers to leave off work at 2pm on a Saturday, the idea being that they would be refreshed and sober enough to start work again on Monday morning. As a consequence, it enabled workers to go off and participate in sporting activities or watch football on a Saturday afternoon, which is why football matches

traditionally kicked off at 3pm on that day. Incidentally, the first use of the term 'weekend', according to the Oxford English Dictionary, was in 1879, when it appeared in a magazine called 'Notes and Queries'.

The opening up of Sundays not only changed the pattern of shopping, but it also gave an impetus to the retail trade in general, which in turn led to an increasing number of new shopping malls and out of town retail parks, The character of our high streets was fast changing too with once familiar shop names disappearing. Looking through David's photos makes you realise just how much change there's been and a reminder of some of those once familiar High Street names that have disappeared. The adverts too are also a reminder of a different age. I'm thinking in particular of the number of products associated with smoking.

David met his future wife, Brenda in 1963, while they were both working at Ilfords at Ilford Broadway. After they married in 1966, they managed to buy a house in Great Cornard, a village on the edge of Sudbury in Suffolk. This meant that David and Brenda had to find new jobs. His interest in buses led him to become a coach driver with Chambers at nearby Bures. From there he later moved to drive with Hedingham & District and Eastern National at Chelmsford. Away from London he now began to photograph buses and coaches in different parts of the country, wherever, in fact, his coach work took him. He visited Blackpool quite a lot, for that was where his mother's parents had moved early in the last war. He loved the trams there and the collection includes many photos of them. By the early 1960s Blackpool was the last outpost of trams in this country.

I mentioned at the start that David grew up on the Becontree Housing Estate. When I was a kid, my dad often took me on train and bus spotting trips to different parts of London, but we never got to Becontree. However, had we chosen, we could have got there directly by one of our local Stoke Newington bus routes, and that was the 106 which ran from Finsbury Park to Becontree, Chittys Lane. I say directly, but a journey to Becontree would have taken us no less than 75 minutes. It was a route basically in two halves with the pivotal point being Poplar and the Docks. The western half from Finsbury

Park threaded its way through Hackney in a south easterly direction. The eastern half from Poplar wended its way north easterly through East Ham, Barking to Becontree. The route stayed basically unchanged from 1934 until 1971, when the route from the Finsbury Park end was cut short to terminate at Whitechapel, and that remains the case today. It was only when I looked up Chittys Lane on the internet that I discovered how significant that road turned out to be. For on No.26 Chittys Lane there is a blue plaque. Normally a blue plaque on a building is there to commemorate the name of a famous person who lived there, but not in this case. The reason for it being here is to mark the first house that was completed on the vast Becontree Housing Estate.

This estate had its origins in the Housing and Town Planning Act of 1919, which permitted the London County Council (L.C.C.) to build housing outside of the County of London for the first time. Over 27,000 new homes were built on 3,000 acres of compulsorily purchased market gardens, fields and lanes in the parishes of Barking, Dagenham and Ilford. Prompting this Act was Lloyd George's 'Homes fit for Heroes' slogan, which in part was a response to and a way of warding off the kind of revolutions recently seen in Russia and Germany.

The estate was designed as a cottage garden one, mainly to rehouse workers being displaced by slum clearances in the East End. The first homes to be completed were on Chittys Lane in 1921. By the time the estate was more or less complete in 1935, it was home to roughly 120,000 people. At the time it was the largest social housing estate in the world. The majority lived in two storey cottages with front and back gardens, two living rooms, a large modern kitchen, bathroom and toilet. For many this would have been the first time they would have lived somewhere with an indoor toilet, and having a bathroom as well would have felt like real luxury. An appearance of uniformity was actually quite deceptive, for there were no less than 91 different housing types. Privet hedges were planted at the front of every garden, with strict rules about keeping the garden neat and tidy, as well as making sure that their children behaved appropriately. To encourage people to keep their gardens neat and tidy, prizes were awarded for the best gardens. To discourage heavy drinking the L.C.C.

refused to build no more than six pubs. In the early years at least, all the prospective tenants were interviewed by L.C.C. officials who then selected the ones they considered the more suitable. By and large the majority of the new tenants came from the relatively prosperous upper working classes. One of the criticisms early on was lack of commercial and social amenities. There was also little work in the area at first until Ford Dagenham arrived in 1931, along with the big chemical company May and Baker. The designers never anticipated that the tenants might one day own cars, so there were no garages or provision for parking, with the result that many of the front gardens have now been replaced with hard-standing for cars and various bins. But in the early 1960s when David was photographing here, the hedges and gardens still looked cared for. I've photographed there a few times, although not recently, and I must say I was quite impressed with what I saw. Finally, I think it's worth mentioning the names of some of people who grew up there, and they include, footballers, Sir Alf Ramsey (Spurs right back and manager of England World Cup winning side in 1966), Sir Bobby Moore (West Ham and England captain of that World Cup winning team), Terry Venables (Spurs and England manager), Jimmy Greaves (Spurs and England forward): comedians, Max Bygraves and Dudley Moore: singer, Sandie Shaw, plus the former Archbishop of Canterbury, George Carey. Formed in 1930 the Dagenham Girl Pipers are still going strong.

Towards the end of his life listening to music and looking through old bus books were a great comfort, until illness denied him even these pleasures. He seemed to have a special affinity with animals. Although he himself had no pets, animals would always take to him. He just had a natural relationship with them. David died on August 7th 2015, leaving behind his widow, Brenda and their two sons, Andrew and Colin.

Finally, I would like to think that this book celebrates and commemorates a small part of David's life. He was undoubtedly a prolific bus photographer and his work deserves to be shared by a wider audience. I would like to thank him in retrospect for the pleasure his photos have left behind.

Pre-war RT86, looking a little careworn after 21 years' service, stands alongside RT53 at Barking garage in June 1960. After withdrawal from regular service in 1955, about 60 of them work as staff buses, while most of the remainder became trainers. Final withdrawal came at the beginning of 1963. The view of RT53 shows the distinctive the rear roof number box, a feature that was not continued once production of the class got underway again in 1947. When they returned to service after the war, the rear roof number box was never used again. Another difference was the slope below the cab window. A more subtle difference was the placing of the destination above the via points. With the post-war RTs, this was placed below them. The pre-war RTs, designated RT2, began entering service in 1939, although strictly speaking only RT1 was actually in service before the war began in the September. It had entered service in the June, working on the 22 route out Putney's Chelverton Road garage. Most of the RT2s were allocated initially to either Chelverton Road or Putney Bridge garage. The remaining few were sent to Gillingham Street garage, Victoria, for service on the 22 and 52. RT2 was completed in September 1939, after which production continued until February 1942 and then ceased for the duration of the war. DGS1-17

RT110 (FXT285) stands waiting in the yard for its next trainee driver in June 1960. Behind it is RT1587, a standard post-war RT, blinded for service on the 87, a route that would take it out to Rainham in Essex, one of the eastern limits of London's red buses. During the war years a number of RT2s sustained bomb damage. In the case of RT110 it resulted in the loss of its front roof box, which for many years gave it a unique appearance. It remained at Chelverton Road garage for virtually all of its service life, and regularly worked the 74 route to Camden Town. Then in 1954, only months before its withdrawal from regular service, it was fitted with a front roof box, albeit a non-standard one. It arrived as a trainer at Barking in December 1959, before moving on to Shepherds Bush garage eight months later. Like the other remaining RT2s, final withdrawal came in early 1963. There was an unexpected twist, though, in the RT2 story, for while most were due for imminent withdrawal, seven were given a reprieve, repainted in green and sent to Hertford garage, specifically to work the 327. They were replacing a batch of post-war STLs which could be sold off. There was an issue with one of the bridges the route crossed. The one in question was the Metropolitan Water Board bridge at Broxbourne, which was not strong enough to carry a standard RT plus its passengers. The seven in question were RT2s 36, 62, 79, 93. 114, 128 and 137, and they were chosen because all of them had only recently received overhauls. They arrived at Herford in May 1955 and stayed there until the end of August 1957, by which time the bridge in question had been reconstructed and was now strong enough to take a standard RT3. I can still remember the excitement of going out to Hertford by the 342 bus from High Barnet to see both the STLs and RT2s. DGS1-18

RT1153 waits in the yard outside Barking Garage ready for its next duty on route 23 in the June of 1960. At this time the 23 ran from Aldgate to Becontree Heath from Monday to Saturday. It was extended during the day to Marylebone from Monday to Friday except evenings. The route required 32 vehicles. Barking supplied 12 RTs, while Poplar provided 20 RMs. RT1153 was one of 250 RTs manufactured by Saunders Engineering on Anglesey and they were numbered 1152-1401. They entered service between November 1948 and September 1950, somewhat later than intended. RT1153 was one of the initial batch that went to Muswell Hill Garage to replace the ageing LTs on the 43 route. Most of the RT bodies were manufactured by either Weymann of Addlestone or Park Royal of West London, but from time to London Transport had to find other body manufacturers because Weymann and Park Royal could not provide enough bodies for the number of chassis arriving, so LT turned to Saunders and Cravens of Sheffield to help out. The Saunders' bodies were almost indistinguishable from the standard model. However, there were two slight differences, the more notable of which was the placing of the offside route indicator panel, which was set further back, and this can be seen in the photo. The other small difference was that the bottom front edge of the cab ran directly across to the radiator. Note the washing hanging in the background. DGS1-21

RM39 stands at the Becontree Heath bus station in 1960. It was one of the early production batch of Routemasters which went to Poplar(PR) garage as part of the trolleybus replacement programme. Stage 4 involved the conversion of trolleybus routes at Poplar and West Ham garages to Routemaster operation, and this was the first such direct replacement and took place in November 1959. The bus will be shortly heading for Aberfeldy Street in Poplar. Poplar Garage was just round the corner in Leven Street. Quite a few of the streets in this area of Poplar have names with a Scottish connection. The reason for this is because they were built on the estate which had been bought by the McIntosh family in 1823. A few streets away from Poplar depot was Atholl Street (another Scottish name) garage coded C. This garage was long associated with the two tunnel routes, the 108 for Blackwell Tunnel and the 82 for Rotherhithe Tunnel. It was scheduled to close to coincide with the trolleybus replacement at Poplar in 1959, but due to a delay in the completion of facilities at Poplar garage, the actual closure didn't take place until May 1961. Poplar Garage opened as a tram depot in 1906, converting to trolleybus operation in 1940. This was the last tram depot to be converted to trolleybus operation. Poplar ran the trolleybus routes 565. 567, 569 and 665, running between Aldgate and Barking along the East India Dock Road, which required a total of 70 vehicles. The garage had a capacity for many vehicles than this and so was often used as a vehicle store. All that remains today of the garage is the brick façade. Although the Routemaster proved ultimately to be a very fine and long-lived vehicle, much admired by enthusiasts today, in its early days in service there were any number of issues that needed to be resolved. DGS1-25

Like the 23 route, the 25 has a long association with East London. Both linked Becontree with Aldgate and the City. While the 23 linked the two via Barking, Canning Town, Poplar and Limehouse, the 25 took a more northern route via Ilford, Stratford, Bow and Mile End. By 1960 the 25 was running between Becontree Heath and Victoria via Aldgate. At the start of that year the route was operated by 60 RTs from Forest Gate (G) garage and by 22 RTLs from Bow. However, in April Forest Gate garage closed and the operation passed to West Ham along with a large part of Forest Gate's allocation of RTs. Since 1993, though, it now has just run between Ilford and Oxford Circus, thus cutting off part of each end of the route. Shortening routes has been a feature of route changes in recent years in an effort to maintain schedules. RT 4795 was one of those RTs transferred to West Ham garage with the closure of Forest Gate. It was new into service at Alperton (ON) garage in 1954. After a three year spell there, it was re-allocated to Forest Gate, before moving on to West Ham. Its 22 year service came to an end at Seven Kings (AP) garage in 1976. It was finally withdrawn from Barking in 1977, having worked there for a short time as a trainer. DGS1-26

RT805 stands at Becontree Heath bus station on a dull day in June 1960 ready to return to the War Memorial. Rainham on route 87. New to Mortlake garage in September 1948 it began work on the 9 route. When in November 1949 RTs replaced LTs at Mortlake on the 73 route RT805 began to work on that too. At the same time Tottenham's allocation on the 73 switched from LT to RTL. I can remember seeing this vehicle passing my home on Stoke Newington Church Street. Visible behind RT805 is Dagenham Town, now the Civic Centre. This grade II liated building is a fine example of 1930s Art Deco architecture. In 1960 the 87 route ran between Rainham and Brentwood via Dagenham, Becontree, Romford, Gidea Park and Harold Wood. DGS1-27

On the same day in June 1960 we see RTL1321 of Bow garage followed by RT3272 of West Ham, both on route 25. They are standing at Becontree Heath bus station while their crews take a break. RTL1321 was one of 1631 RTLs introduced between 1948 and 1954 and built on the Leyland PD2 Titan chassis . Their bodies were interchangeable with most RTs. The main visual difference was the traditional Leyland style radiator. The first one, RTL501, appeared in the spring of 1948 and was unique for many years in having a rooftop body. Park Royal was the main supplier of RTL bodies. Their life span was almost half that of the RTs. The last 60 or so spent nearly four years in store at Garston and Reigate garages. I remember seeing about 50 of them stored at the back of Garston garage in 1957. By the time they entered service in 1958 many of the earlier RTLs were being withdrawn following the service cuts in the autumn of that year. Quite a few were sold to Ceylon (now Sri Lanka). RTL1321 had only just returned from overhaul at Aldenham. After overhaul it was transferred from Dalston (D) garage to Bow (BW). The vehicle behind, RT3272, was one of the many RTs transferred across to West Ham (WH) after the closure of Forest Gate garage two months before this photo was taken.DGS1-30

To meet the urgent need for new buses in the immediate post-war period London Transport introduced two single deck models. The first of these was the A.E.C Regal 14T12 T class which went into service in earl 1946, with 50 of the 80 vehicles going to the Central area. Later that year 31 of the Leyland Tiger PS1 model, classified as the TD class, arrived to take up duty at Muswell Hill (MH) garage for 212, the short 16 minute run between Muswell Hill and Finsbury Park. Two years later a further 100 were introduced. Unlike TD1-31, which had Weymann bodies very similar to the 14T12 Ts, TD32-131 had Mann Egerton ones. The Weymann bodies on the T and TD had an overhanging destination box above the cab, which gave them something of a scowling look. Mann Egerton dispensed with this feature and had a straight roofline above the cab and this tended to give them a more modern look. The TD was basically the single deck version of the successful and influential Leyland STD. TD101, seen here on the forecourt in front of Edgware Underground station. TD101 spent its entire service life at Edgware working on the 240/240A and 251 routes. It was introduced in May 1949 and withdrawn in October 1962. The TDs at Edgware were the last of the class in service in London. Their replacement came in the form of Regal IV RFs. When the route was introduced in 1947 it only ran between Edgware and Bunns Lane, Page Street and was operated by 3 pre-war LTL 'Scooters', the single deck version of the LT, one of the standard double deck London buses of the 1930s. The route was extended to Mill Hill East station in 1951, requiring a further 5 TDs. When this photo was taken in 1960 the allocation had increased to 10. DGS06-2

Parked up in Cromwell Road, Kingston is a line of four TDs headed by an RF. The rear vehicle is TD126 blinded for route 215. The other TD routes operated from Kingston garage in 1960 were the 201 to Hampton Court via Surbiton, the 216 and 218 to Staines and the 219 to Weybrisge, while nearby Norbiton garage ran the 264 to Hersham. The date is not given, but judging by the trees it looks to be some time in the winter of 1960/1, and judging by the absence of traffic it could be a Sunday. Cromwell Road today is much busier today, as it forms part of the one-way system taking traffic heading in the Central London direction. To the left of the buses is where the present day Kingston bus station lies. The pre-war 215 route ran all the way out to Guildford. Gradually over the years the route has been cut, but the route has always covered the section between Kingston and Esher. In 1960 the route ran as far as Ripley. In 1988 the route was renumbered to K3 and today runs beyond Kingston and terminates now at Roehampton Asda. During their 14 year lifespan, the majority of TDs spent at least part their working service in the Kingston area working from either Kingston or Norbiton garages. DGS06-6

On the same day as the previous photo RF346 from Sutton (A) garage is seen near the entrance to Kingston garage, ready to set off back to Belmont. The 213 route ran from Kingston to Belmont from the start of the London Transport era in 1934 until January 1962. However, the core of the route between Kingston and Sutton has remained unchanged right through to the present day. LTL 'scooters' had operated the route from 1934 until late 1952. After that RFs began arriving but it was not until May 1953 that the switch from LTL to RF was completed. Thanks in particular to Alan Cross the LTLs on the 213 have been well documented in photo. The work on lowering of the road beneath the railway bridge at Worcester Park station finished in May 1963 and this allowed double-deckers to be used for the first time on this busy route. From then until the route was converted to One Person Operation in August 1970 the route was scheduled to be run by RTs, although Norbiton RMs occasionally made an appearance. The first OPO vehicles were the DMS class. Kingston was a fascinating place to visit in the mid 1950s for it was the last place to see the post-war Regal Ts, some of which were still in green after having been drafted in from the Country area. DGS06-10

RM19 is pictured about to turn into the former West Ham garage after finishing its turn on the short run between Dagenham East station and Dagenham Ford Works. These journeys were separate from the main 25 route which ran from Becontree Heath to Victoria. It was introduced in November 1958, replacing the experimental 193. West Ham and Poplar garages were the first to receive the production batch of Routemasters. During the transition phase between electric and diesel traction which took place between November 1959 and April 1960 at West Ham, the Routemasters worked on trolleybus routes like the 689/690. When they arrived at West Ham in November 1959 they worked on the new 5 route, the replacement for the trolleybus routes 565/567/665. No date is given for this photo, but I am assuming it was taken during that transition period. Officially the Routemasters didn't replace the RTs on the 25 route until 1972, but clearly they sometimes appeared on the peak hour only Dagenham Fords runs. Although the Routemasters proved to be a very successful and long lived vehicle, there were a number of issues concerning that early batch and they were sent back for modification, and replaced by later models. DGS06-21

TD105 on the 240A stands alongside two RTs on the 107A on the forecourt of Edgware Underground station in the summer of 1960. The two RTs originally had Park Royal bodies without a front roof route number box, but RT2824 on the right has acquired a different body during overhaul. The 240A route was introduced in 1947 using three pre-war single decker LTL 'Scooters'. From 1949 TDs started appearing on the route as well. When the route was extended to Mill Hill East station in 1951 and a Sunday service introduced, the TDs were left in sole charge of the operation. The weekday allocation increased to nine vehicles. The TDs remained on the route until 1962, making them the last of the class in London service. They were replaced by RFs, but their stay on the route only lasted until 1966. The route then became a Sundays only operation and extended beyond Mill Hill East to Golders Green using RTs from Edgware. The final change of vehicle type came in 1971 when SMS 'Swifts' took over. In 1979 the route was withdrawn and replaced by extending the 221 and restoring its daily link to Edgware, which has continued to the present day. DGS06-22-

RT2756 from Enfield garage is working on the 107A, which runs from Edgware to Enfield Lock. It is standing on the forecourt of Edgware Underground station. The route was shared between Enfield and Edgware garages, and it meandered across the northern perimeter of London, passing through Borehamwood, Barnet, Cockfosters, Oakwood and Enfield. DGS06-24

RM12 is about to enter WH garage in Greengate Street soon after the departure of the last trolleybuses in April 1960. The overhead wires are still partially in place, the wires being. The 249A was one of the routes replacing the 687 trolleybus route. At the time of this photo was taken the route ran from Chingford, Royal Forest Hotel to Victoria & Albert Docks M-F (except evenings) & Saturday. On Sundays it just ran from the Docks as far as Chingford Mount. In October 1961 it became a Sunday only route running between the Docks and Chingford Mount. During the week a revised 41 route replaced it over the stretch between Stratford and the Docks, while the rest was covered by a strengthened 249. Until 1966 it had an RM operated route, but in February 1966 RMLs took over. However, the route was withdrawn two years later in September 1968, replaced by the 69 and a new 241 route. RM12 was new into service at West Ham in November 1959, working on the 5 and 238 routes. The early production batch of RMs starting with RM5 was not in service before they were taken off the road because of a suspected steering column defect. Many were off the road for nearly two years, not returning to service until May 1962. Despite this RM12 was in London Transport for a further 16 years, before being sold to Southend Transport where it became their No.101, going to spend another 5 years with them.
DGS06-30

Passing Shepherds Bush Green is class K2 trolleybus 1240 heading to Clapham Junction on the 628. This route was operated from Hammersmith(HB) depot and ran from Craven Park, Harlesden to Clapham Junction with an allocation of 22 vehicles (M-F), jointly with the M-F peak hours 626 which through to Acton Market Place. The 626 and 628 pair of routes were replaced by the 268 with RMs from Shepherds Bush (S) garage, when the depot at Hammersmith closed in July 1960. The 268 itself only lasted until the last day of 1966. The section between Scrubs Lane and Willesden Junction was covered by an extension of the 220. The K class with 325 vehicles was the largest of the trolleybus classes. The K1 and K2 sub classes had 150 in each. The final K3 batch had 25. All entered service between 1938 and 1940. Externally the Ks were almost identical, except that the K3s had sidelights projecting from the front panel instead of from the body sides. What divided the sub classes were the controllers, with the K1s having Metrovick ones, whereas the K2s and K3s had English Electric. Both the chassis and the body on the Ks were built by Leyland. DGS07-01

L3 1429 is entering Aldgate bus station after completing its journey from Tottenham Court Road, Maple Street. This inner orbital route might have been almost a complete circle had LPTB secured permission to extend the overhead wires through to Bedford Square, but the same forces that prevented the trams from entering either the City or the West End prevailed once more. The route was operated from Highgate (HT) depot with an allocation of 49 vehicles M-F. Divided into three sub-classes the L was the second largest class of trolleybus with 170 vehicles, although three were destroyed during the war. Following the success of the experimental chassisless trolleybus 754, LT opted for this design with the L class. Without the weight of a conventional chassis, the saving weight could be used to strengthen the bodywork in order to prolong the vehicle's life. When Highgate depot changed over to diesel traction in February 1961, the only change to the route was its renumbering to 253. Then for twenty six years it was operated by Routemasters from Highgate, Edmonton, Stamford Hill, Clapton, Dalston and Ash Grove, before becoming OPO in November 1987. DGS07-5

With the effects of wartime damage in the background RF16 waits to return to Harlow on Green Line route 720A. The first 25 RFs were designed for private hire work, entering service in May 1951 just in time for the Festival of Britain. Their distinctive feature was the glazed cant panels in the side of the roof. While the first fifteen remained on private hire work in London, RF16-25 were converted to Green Line service in 1956. The 720A was introduced in July 1954 to run from Aldgate to Harlow Town Centre, and it was the first Green Line route to serve a new town. It ran hourly using 3 RFs from Epping (EP) garage. In October 1962 double deck RMC Routemasters entered service allowing the former private hire RFs to be withdrawn. May 1963 saw the opening of a new and much larger garage at nearby Harlow (HA), and this led to the closure of the one at Epping and the transfer of routes and vehicles there. With the introduction of the new Green Line 717 route from Welwyn Garden City to Wrotham, the 8 RMCs at Harlow for the 720/720A were transferred to Hatfied (HF) and Swanly (SJ) garages with each receiving four, and RFs returned to run the 720/720A routes again. Finally in October 1965 the 720A was withdrawn and the 720 was diverted to run into the centre of Harlow en route to Bishop Stortford. RF16 later moved to the Irish Republic. It was subsequently brought back to England in 1992 and has been undergoing restoration work ever since. Photo taken in July 1960. DGS07-6

J3 1047 is seen leaving Moorgate, Finsbury Square heading for Highgate Village on route 611. The route was operated solely from Highgate depot, and the vehicles, whether tram or trolleybus, were always specially adapted braking systems for the long, steep climb from the Archway up Highgate Hill to reach Highgate Village. The J3s were a small sub-class of J class and Highgate depot had a long association with that class. 1047 entered service from there in May 1939 and was still there right up until depot switched from electric to diesel traction in February 1961 even though the 611 route for which it was intended had switched over to diesel in July 1960.. All three J sub-classes had an A.E.C. chassis, but whereas the J1 and J2s had Metro-Cammell bodies, the J3s were bodied by BRCW. Finsbury Square was developed between 1777 and 1791 on land that had once been a green space known as Finsbury Fields. Until the late 19th century it would have looked like any other Georgian square in London with tall terraced hosing surrounding a central communal garden. Gradually from that time the houses started to be demolished to be replaced by large scale commercial properties, so completely changing the character of the square. A drinking fountain was added to the square, commemorating Tom Smith, the inventor of the Christmas cracker. DGS07-9

1047 is pictured again the same day in July 1960 at the Highgate Village terminus in company this time with L1 1356. The L1 was a small sub-class of just 14 vehicles, specifically designed for working on steep hills like the J3s. When buses took over from the trolleybuses in July 1962, the route was renumbered to become the 271. The actual route itself remained unchanged. Later on there were a couple of weekend extensions to Hendon Central and Liverpool Street bus station. When the route was withdrawn in May 2023 it had been back to its original one since 2003. The route's replacement was partly done by diverting the 21 at Moorgate to cover the section from there to Holloway and by rerouting the 263 to run from Highbury Barn to Barnet via Highgate Hill, Highgate village and North Hill Road instead of Archway Road. Highgate Village still retains much of its Georgian heritage and character. It's somewhat surprising to learn how many of these 'villages' there are to be found in London, Places like Highgate have remained largely untouched and still have a special atmosphere. Highgate was once on the main road leading north out of London, hence the number of old pubs on the High Street that stem from the stage coach era. DGS07-11

K1 1071 calls at Hammersmith Broadway on a 630 to West Croydon. I think this photo was taken where Butterwick is today, and would have been taken shortly before the Hammersmith (HB) depot closed in July 1960. Running between Harlesden College Park the 630 was the longest daily trolleybus route. However the peak hours M.-F. 655 service between Acton Vale and Clapham Junction was even longer. College Park was actually the name of a pub on the corner of Harrow Road and Scrubs Lane. The trolleybuses terminated in Letchford Gardens, a turning off the Harrow Road, still some way short of Willesden Junction station. As well as the 630, Hammersmith depot also operated the 626 and 628. The 630 served two sports stadia, White City and Wimbledon. For the latter a road (Summerstown) was specifically wired up to serve the greyhound stadium. On race nights the blind read 'Summerstown' to avoid confusion with the Wimbledon tennis club. The 630 was replaced by the 220 using new Routemasters from Shepherds Bush garage. In the background is a Royal London office building. 1071 is advertising the Starlight Special train service that ran from 1953 until about1960. Apparently it didn't appear in the May 61 issue of Bradshaw. It ran a Friday night service from London Marylebone and either Glasgow St Enoch or Edinburgh Princes Street with the train dividing at Carstairs. The price was 85 shillings for a return ticket, which in today's money would be £4.25. DGS07-14.

K2 1178 turns into what is now Butterwick on Hammersmith Broadway on the 628 bound for Clapham Junction. On leaving Hammersmith Broadway the trolleybus will pass under the Hammersmith Flyover, which at the time (1960) was yet to be completed, and then head south along Fulham Palace Road towards Putney. It was the building of the flyover that caused the closure of Hammersmith depot earlier than planned. The buildings on the left have all been demolished and replaced by Hammersmith bus station, part of which sits on top of the Metro Centre, the modern shopping mall, below which is the District and Piccadilly line Underground station. The coach behind is one of Banfields Coaches' Leyland Royal Tigers. The company was founded in 1928 by Michael Banfield. When this photo was taken in July 1960, the company was based at the former LT Nunhead (AH) garage in Nunhead Lane. They ran excursions to seaside resorts on the Kent and Sussex coasts among other things. Were the two young boys bus spotting out to witness the final days of the trolleybuses from Hammersmith depot? DGS07-15

By the mid-1950s the last of the pre-war types had disappeared from the streets of London and the early post-war STD would soon follow suit too. That left the 76 lowbridge RLHs as the only double deck variant to the RT family, and that made them seem somewhat special to young bus spotters like myself. The three routes they worked on at the time were near or on the periphery of London and very distant from each other. RLH76, seen here, was the last one in the class. Coming into service in 1952 it had two spells at both Merton and Hornchurch, before spending its final four years at Dalston on the 178. Here it stands at the Upminster station terminus in Hall Lane. In the background is Upminster Methodist Church, built in 1923 in the Tudor Gothic style. Behind the bus is a monkey puzzle tree (araucaria araucana), a conifer tree dating back over 200 million years and so earlier than the dinosaurs. Native to Chile, the first on arrived here in 1775. It was sometimes planted near a church because there was a rumour that it could prevent the Devil from entering bodies during burial. In 1960, when this photo was taken, the 248 ran between Upminster and Cranham via St Mary's Lane. It was a low bridge carrying the Upmister-Grays branch line over St May's Lane that necessitated the use of RLHs. At that time this short route only required three RLHs. Prior to the RLHs taking over in 1955, the route had been run by single deck TDs (1948-55) and Ts (1936- 48).When the RLHs were withdrawn in 1970, they were replaced by new SMS Swifts and the route was extended to Romford. DGS07-19

Highgate depot's L2 1372 is leaving Cambridge Heath Road and turning into Whitechapel Road and so the final stage of its run to Aldgate. The photo was taken in January 1961 just weeks before stage 9 of the trolleybus conversion would take place on 1st February when all the remaining trolleybus routes out of Highgate would switch from electric to diesel. The wires for the two trolleybus routes, the 661 and 663, heading east to the right along the Mile End Road have already been dismantled. Bow depot operated both these routes, plus the 695 Bow-Chadwell Heath service and that was part of the stage 3 conversion in August 1959. The L1 sub-class consisted of just nine vehicles was identical to the L1s, except that they didn't have the special braking equipment needed for hilly routes. DGS10-58

I think the high wall beside K1 1068 could be the rear of the former Finsbury Park Odeon cinema, which was situated on the corner of Seven Sisters and Isledon Road. After 1956 the cinema had a thirty year spell as a famous rock music venue. Since 1988 it has been a Brazilan Pentecostal church. This would then place the scene in Coleridge Road. Today Isledon Road is part of a one-way traffic system between Finsbury Park and Camden Road, Holloway prison. The other trolleybus in the distance turning into Coleridge Road from Seven Sisters could well be L3 1384. Both vehicles are presumably working shorts from Aldgate. A smartly dressed bus inspector is approaching the L3 to have word with the driver. Battery driven milk floats were a common feature of the day when most people had milk delivered to their doorstep. The two alcoholic drinks being advertised on 1068, VAT 69 Blended Scotch Whisky and Myers Rum are still with us today, more than sixty years later. DGS10-68

David began his bus photography in 1960 just in time to catch many of the trolleybus routes before their conversion to diesel. The Tally Ho at North Finchley was an excellent venue with no fewer than seven routes converging here. L3 1431 has just completed its journey on the 517 up from Kings Cross, which indicates it is a Sunday. Also the absence of people and the shops being closed are further evidence. Behind the 517 is another L3 1466, this time on the 521. Both routes terminated at High Holborn M.-Sat., the 517 taking the more direct route via East Finchley, Archway and Holloway, whereas the 521 went via New Southgate, Wood Green, Manor House and Finsbury Park. The two routes converged at Holloway, Nags Head and from then on they followed the same route via Caledonian Road, Kings Cross and Grays Inn Road. When this photo was taken in January 1960 the route was only weeks away from conversion. The 517 and 617 were replaced by RMs on the 17 and they continued to be run by Highgate. The only change to the route was a M.-Sat. extension to Camberwell Green. DGS10-72

K2 1169 on route 659 is seen at Holborn Circus in January 1961. The 659 was another long route, running from Waltham Cross on the northern edge of the central area through to Holborn Circus. The route was operated by Edmonton (EM) depot, which was shortly going to switch over to diesel as part of the stage 10 conversion programme in April 1961. Six months earlier the railway network in the area had switched from steam to electric traction. The bronze equestrian statue behind the trolleybus is that of Albert, the Prince Consort. Erected in 1874 by the City of London as an official tribute to Queen Victoria's late husband. Placed in the centre of Holborn Circus, the statue proved to be a hazard to motorists by obstructing their sight lines. Due to being a noted accident black spot, the statue was finally moved in 2012 and placed at the side out of harm's way where it could be seen much better anyway. Albert fared much better than King George IV, whose statue at a similar five-way junction at Kings Cross was unceremoniously pulled down in 1842. DGS11-12.

David returned to Kingston on another Sunday, this time in early 1961 to record the remaining TDs allocated to Kingston. Seen here is TD54 blinded for the 215, the only route in the area at the time still operating with TDs. It heads a line of four other TDs with an RF bringing up the rear. The 215 finally converted to RF in March 1962. TD54 was one of the first batch of TDs introduced in 1946. After spells at Hornchurch (RD) garage for the 248, 250 and 252 routes and Edgware for the 240/240A, it arrived at Kingston in 1958 and finished its days there in 1962. DGS11-15

It is another Sunday on a dismal winter's day in January 1960. It is just weeks away from stage 5 of the conversion programme at the beginning of February, which saw the end of trolleybuses at West Ham depot. Stage 4, the previous November, had seen the earlier conversion of West Ham's other routes, these being the 567,569 and 665. This line of three L3s is headed by 1529, the final member of this sub-class. Behind it are 1390 on the 669 and 1440 on the 689. The 689 and the 690 were two relatively short local routes running from Stratford Broadway to East Ham, where they did a circular route around Plashet Grove, High Street North, Barking Road and Green Street. Not particularly busy during the week, these two routes came alive on Saturdays with shoppers and football fans travelling to and from Upton Park for West Ham's home matches. After conversion they became the 162 route. DGS11-17

The conversion programme to diesel at Highgate depot took place over stages 7, 9 and 10.Stage 7 in July 1960 saw just one conversion, that of the 611.The bulk of the changes occurred in the stage 9 programme of February 1961. That left just the 627 (M.-Sat.) and their Sunday only allocation on the 609 running under the wires at Highgate depot. The main allocation on the 609 was the responsibility of Finchley (FY) depot and that was not due to convert until the stage 12 programme in November 1961. So between April 30th and November 5th 1961 the route had the unique distinction of having 5 Routemasters from Highgate running alongside Finchley's trolleybuses on a Sunday. In this photo Highgate's L3 1424 pulls into the Tally Ho bus station at North Finchley ready for the return trip to Moorgate shortly before the stage 9 conversion. Only a few of the Highgate trolleybuses reached the final destination of Barnet Church; most of them stopped short here at the Tally Ho. The well-known Tally Ho public house is just to the right along Ballards Lane. The pub took its name from the Tally Ho Corner, where three major roads converged, Ballards Lane, High Road and Woodhouse Road. That, in turn, derived its name from the Tally Ho Coach company which supplied horse for the first change on the Birmingham Mail coach. DGS12A-3

This is the entrance to Highgate depot shortly before the stage 9 programme in February in 1961. Two sets of tram tracks are visible, set among the cobblestones. A pole used to raise the trolley poles back up to the overhead wires is propped up against the entrance wall. The nearest of the trolleybuses seen in the line is L3 1388, blinded for the 653. The depot was always known as Holloway up until 1950, at which point it was renamed 'Highgate' to avoid confusion with the nearby Holloway (J) bus garage. When the latter closed in September 1971, it resumed its former name of Holloway. Highgate and West Ham were the two largest trolleybus garages in London. Holloway, too, was one of the largest bus garages. It was where my father worked as a driver for fifteen years. The entrance to Highgate depot is in Pemberton Gardens, a wide tree lined avenue off the west side of Holloway Road. The exit on Pemberton Terrace facing Monnery Road. Holloway bus garage was situated on the east side of Holloway Road a little further down towards the Nags Head, lying between Fortnam and Kingsdown Roads. Originally it had been a horse bus depot, so it showed none of the symmetry of the tram one. It was a garage that didn't lack character, and despite its slightly ramshackle appearance, it was still one of the largest bus garages in London. DGS12A-7

K2 1323 stands in Maple Street waiting to set off back to Enfield on route 629, a route operated from Wood Green depot. This is the closest either the trams or trolleybuses ever got to the West End. Going back to the days of the horse trams in late 19th century there was a prejudice in this part of London against first tram tracks and then against electric traction of any sort. Maple Street was formerly known as London Street. The change of name, I assume, was connected to the proximity of the large Maple & Co. the upmarket furniture and upholstery store on Tottenham Court Road, founded in 1841 by John Maple. This part of London received extensive bombing during the war and the area looked down at heel and bomb sites were still a fairly common site in London even by the early 1960s. What was left of these once fine Georgian streets look drab and unwelcoming. There seemed an absence or lack of colour everywhere, and especially so in winter. Conversion to diesel of the 629 came with stage 10 in late April 1961. The only change was the route number to 269 and new Routemaster RMs to replace the trolleybuses. The route only lasted till 1968, when it was replaced the a strengthened 29 and the new W4 MBS operated route from Turnpike Lane to Enfield. DGS12A-10

London Memories

Left. RTL419 on route 42 stands at an almost deserted Aldgate bus station in early January 1961. For 55 years between 1939 and 1994 the 42 ran almost unaltered from Aldgate to Camberwell Green. Currently it has a short extension from Aldgate on to Liverpool Street, terminating in Worship Street. At the other end it extends beyond Camberwell Green down to East Dulwich, Sainsburys. RTL419 entered service in late 1949 working from Turnham Green (V) garage. It transferred to Camberwell (Q) garage in 1960, and after a four year spell there, it was withdrawn and sold to the Ceylon (Sri Lanka) Transport Board. Camberwell garage has had a long association with this route. RTLs began working on this route in 1954 and stayed on it until 1966, making them the class with the longest association with the route. Before the RTLs, SRTs operated the route between 1951 and 1954. The SRTs had RT bodies but an older STL chassis, which tended to make their performance rather sluggish. Along with the 78 route these routes having been crossing Tower Bridge for almost 90 years. DGS12A-15

Right. RT3238 on route 722 to Upminster, Corbets Tey is standing at Aldgate bus station. Before the war buses terminating in the centre of Upminster had long been a problem. The solution was to extend the Y2 (post war 722) through to Corbets Tey. In July 1950 a batch of brand new RTs numbered 3224-3259 was sent to Romford London Road (RE) garage to replace the STLs and D class wartime Daimlers on the buses 721 and 722 routes. These RTs had no advertisements and on the sides between the decks was a Green Line metal bullseye. When the Dartford Tunnel was opened in November 1963, the 722 was extended through it to Dartford. Patronage was very poor though, so it was withdrawn exactly a year later. The last double-deckers to serve the route were the RCL Routemasters, which arrived in in July 1965. DGS12A-17

RT3245 is parked up at Aldgate bus station waiting to return to Brentwood. The destination in Brentwood being Highwood Hospital indicates that it is a Sunday working. The RTs arrived at London Road garage for the 721 and 722 in July 1950, replacing the STLs and utility Daimlers, neither of which were up to Green Line standards in terms of comfort. Although an improvement, the same could said of the RTs. It was only when the RCL Routemasters took over in June 1965 that the passengers on the721 and 722 routes could experience the standard of comfort other Green Line passengers had come to expect. Sadly that experience was not to last too long, for in 1973 Leyland National LNCs replaced the Routemasters. Plastic seating and spartan interiors were the new order. It was a retrograde step and one that spelled the end for what had once been the busiest Green Line route with a bus every ten minutes. The route was withdrawn in 1977 and with that London Road garage in Romford closed in the July of that year. In many ways the 721 routes foreshadow the present Superloop scheme. DGS12A-18

RT4492 is captured at Aldgate bus station in July 1961 on the 723A to Grays. The 723A was introduced in July 1952 to serve the newly built Belhus Park Estate near Aveley. It continued on to Grays via North Stifford. The 723 reached Grays from Aveley via Purfleet and South Stifford. Both routes had two buses an hour, and both, to begin with, ran through from Grays to Tilbury. TFs then RFs ran the route until July 1954, when a new batch of 21 RTs were introduced. They were identical to the earlier batch of RTs at Romford for the 721 and 722 routes, with no adverts and a Green Line bullseye on both sides between the two decks. In July 1965 the RTs gave way to new RCL Routemasters. DGS12A-19

Most London bus routes have seen changes over the years. While some have been remarkably stable, this has not been the case for certain route numbers. Since 1934 there have been four different iterations of the 48 and 70 routes, while for the 26 there have been no less than five. The version seen here is the third. It was introduced in August 1959 as a direct replacement for the 661 trolleybus which ran from Aldgate to Leyton (Lea Bridge depot). Bow continued to operate the route, only now with RTLs instead of trolleybuses. Leyton (T) garage also helped out on a Saturday with four of their RTs. In 1964 the roles were reversed and Leyton took over the bulk of the operation. This lasted only a couple of years and the route was withdrawn on the last day of 1966, to be replaced by the new 262 which covered the route between Stratford and Leyton Green. RTWs arrived at Bow with the closure of nearby Old Ford, Clay Hall (CL) garage in November 1959. RTW149 arrived at Bow in November 1960 after overhaul and spent over three years there, normally working on the 8, which Bow inherited from Clay Hall. After 1964 it spent four years as a trainer. Being eight foot wide they were an ideal preparation for driving the new Routemasters of the same width. DGS12A-21

A line of six RTs wait outside the Ford Dagenham works ready to bring the workers home. Leading the line is RT3306, an Upton Park (U) garage vehicle at the time (1961). The other routes terminating there would have been the 87 to Becontree, Romford and Brentwood, the 148 to Becontree, Ilford, Wanstead and Leytonstone, and the 175 to Becontree Romford, Collier Row and Stapleford Abbotts. All served the huge Becontree Housing Estate, at one time the largest in the world. Fords arrival in Dagenham in 1931, plus the large chemical company of May and Baker, gave a big boost to employment in the area. In its heyday in the 1950s more than 40,000 people worked there at Ford. All that's now left is the Engine Plant and the Dagenham Diesel Centre. A large part is being developed for much needed new housing.The 145 seen here will be heading off to the Royal Forest Hotel at Chingford on the edge of Epping Forest. The route took it through Becontree, Ilford, Gants Hill and Woodford. Barking (BK) garage also contributed RTs to the 145. DGS12A-23

Enfield € garage's RT2283 is on a Sunday working of the 242 in May 1961. On a Sunday the route ran from Epping Forest, Wake Arms to Cuffley station, but during the week it continued on beyond Cuffley to Potters Bar and South Mimms. Later that October this Sunday working of the 242 would be replaced by the 205A and the 242A. The former would cover the route from the Wake Arms to Waltham Cross and the latter from Waltham Cross to Potters Bar. RT2283 is pictured here at the Wake Arms terminus. This famous public house had been here seen at least the 18th century, for it had associations with the highwayman, Dick Turpin. The pub belonged to the Wake family who claimed descent from Hereward the Wake, the Wake meaning the last of the Saxons. Although it was situated in the middle of Epping Forest, it was also at the meeting point of roads coming out of north east London, heading north towards Epping and Ongar. The pub was demolished in the 1980s. Enfield ran the route from 1934 until 1963. Since then it has been the responsibility of Potters Bar. RTs operated the route from 1953 until 1968. Before that it had been single deck Ss, Ts and TDs. DGS14-24

London Memories

Two of Edmonton (EM) depot's vehicles are pictured here, K1 1149 and P1 1708, working on the 679 and 659 respectively. They await their next duty at the Waltham Cross terminal on Eleanor Cross Road. The conductor on the 659 has yet to change the blind to Holborn Circus. The inspector is having a word with the driver of 1149 before it heads off to Smithfield. The P1 was a small class of 25 vehicles. They had a Leyland chassis married to an M.C.W. body. They were similar in appearance to the L3 class. Perhaps owing to their extra 6 hundredweight , the P1s had the reputation of being one of the smoothest running of all the trolleybuses in London. They came into service in March 1941. Although a war-time product, they were built entirely to pre-war standards. They were, in fact, the last of the pre-war designs. The class had a long association with Edmonton depot. Both these two routes, along with the 627, last ran on April 25th 1961. David took this photo just two days before this date. The 679 route normally terminated at Enfield garage near Ponders End, but on a Sunday it had an extension to Waltham Cross. DGS18-2

A pair of K2s 1236 and 1182 stand in Eleanor Cross Road ready to depart for Smithfield and Holborn Circus. David gets a friendly thumbs-up greeting from the elderly driver. I wonder if he made the transition to the new diesels coming in. The 679 will shortly become the 279, while the 659 will become the 259. Both will be operated by new Routemasters. Three of Edmonton's four routes, the 627, the 659 and the 679, were part of the stage 10 conversion programme in April 1961. The other Edmonton route, the 649, converted to diesel with the stage 11 programme on the 19th July 1961 along with the Stamford Hill depot's routes, which included a small allocation on the 649. Between April and July of that year Edmonton depot had a mixture of trolleybuses and Routemasters. Ten years before Dad and I had taken the 649 from Stoke Newington all the way up to Waltham Cross. I remember it seemed a very long journey. On the way I started feeling sick, so we got off at Ponders End and caught the train from there back to Clapton. I still have the platform ticket we collected from Ponders End that day and it's dated 21st December 1951. DGS18-6

Certain route numbers seemed to have relatively short lives and the 48 was certainly one of these. There have been four versions of the 48 since 1934, and the first three barely made it to six years. The last one, though, from Whipps Cross then Walthamstow Central to London Bridge survived fifty one years from 1968 until 2019. The version seen here is the third one, introduced in November 1959 as a partial replacement of the trolleybus routes (565,567,569 & 665) along the Commercial Road between Poplar and Aldgate. At first the new 48 ran from Waterloo to Poplar, Blackwall Tunnel with an extension to North Woolwich in rush hour and at the weekends. In 1961 the route lost the Aldgate to Waterloo section and with that Poplar's allocation of Routemasters shrank from 15 to 7. Finally the route was withdrawn in January 1965, replaced by the 40A M-F and by the 40B on Saturday. RM39 spent much of its 25 year career working from garages in East London. DGS21-28

Originally the 56 ran from Aldgate to Limehouse, the down the west side of the Isle Of Dogs along West Ferry Road, terminating at Cubitt Town's Stebondale Street off Manchester Road near the southern tip of the Isle. From 1942 the route was altered to run between Limehouse, Eastern Hotel and Poplar, Blackwall Tunnel. Basically the 56 now just ran round the perimeter of the Isle and it stayed like this until withdrawal in 1969. For such a relatively short route an allocation of 20 vehicles must have meant a very frequent service. For many years it was the only route on the Isle. Until the garage closed in 1959 it had always been operated from Poplar (C) garage, with Old Ford, Clay Hall (CL) helping out at the weekend. From 1950 until 1968 it was operated by RTLs. Only in its final year did it see a switch to RTs. After Poplar, Atholl Street garage closed the other Poplar garage (the former trolleybus depot)took over the route. RTL389 heads a line of five vehicles in what I think is Robin Hood Lane beside the road leading down to Blackwall Tunnel. The second vehicle looks to be on route 15 bound for Kew Green. If this is the case, then it must be a Sunday. The final two vehicles are RMs on the 48. The buildings in the background, on this bleak, damp February day in 1961, look like Victorian tenements buildings. DGS21-29

London Memories

Qi 1838 stands at the Hampton Court terminus of the 667 on Hampton Court Road. Beyond it on the right is The Green, where in July the annual Hampton court Flower Show is held. The Q1 was the only class of trolleybus to be built after the war for London Transport. The original order was 75 vehicles, 60 to replace the ageing Diddlers and 15 to make good the number lost in the war. Two more were added for the couple that had burnt out in fog. They were due to be delivered in November 1946, but in the end because of shortages they didn't start entering service until February 1948.They were an immediate success, popular with both staff and passengers. According to Ken Blacker they were 'fast, smooth and comfortable.Initially they all went to Fulwell (FW) and Isleworth (IH) depot. Later a few were transferred over to Hanwell (HL) depot for the 607. The 667 was operated from Fulwell depotv and ran to Hammersmith via Hampton, Twickenham, Brentford, Chiswick, Turnham Green and Stamford Brook. The 667 and the trolleybuses from Fulwell were part of the stage 14 conversion programme in May 1962. That brought to an end 31 years of trolleybus operation in London. The 667 was replaced by the 267 using Routemasters . The route itself remained unaltered. DGS21-31

Normally one would have expected to see one of Fulwell's Q1s on the 604, but once it became known that London Transport intended to dispose of all of its trolleybuses, a good offer came in from Spain for some of the Q1s. This offer was accepted and they were sold off to nine different Spanish operators. As a result a batch of L3 trolleybuses was drafted into Fulwell to fill the gap. In this photo L3 1396 is seen in Wimbledon amid buildings clad in Portland Stone. The old part of Wimbledon lies to the west at the top of Wimbledon Hill. The newer part grew up around the station, which was opened in 1838 by the London and Southampton Railway. The name Wimbledon means Wynnman's Hill. In Gaelic 'dun' means a hill. DGS21-30

Fulwell's Q1 1839 has just started on its short journey on the 667 to Twickenham. Behind it is Hampton Court Palace. The inner pair of wires would be used by the trolleybuses on the 604 heading back towards Kingston. The 604 terminated on Vrow Walk to the left of this picture. This is February 1961. Like the batch of trolleybuses meant for South Africa, that ended up in Ilford because of the war, the Q1s were also 8 foot wide. The maximum width for buses had previously been set at 7 foot 6 inches. However, from now on 8 foot was to become the norm. The extra six inches on the Q1s allowed the seats to be an inch wider and added four inches to width of the gangway. DGS21-35

A damp, murky day in April 1961 sees Isleworth (IH) depot's Q1 1790 progressing along Shepherds Bush Green Road south side. Isleworth only operated this one route, the 657, which ran between Hounslow and Shepherds Bush. With a requirement for just 30 vehicles, only Lea Bridge was a smaller dept. Until 1950 the depot had been known as Hounslow. Like Fulwell it was a depot that operated Q1s. After some of them had been sold off to Spain, surplus Leyland K1s were drafted in as a replacement. Fulwell and Isleworth were the last two depots to convert to diesel, and this took place in May 1961. The 657 was replaced by the 117 M-Sat, the route being extended from Hounslow through to Shepherds Bush. On a Sunday the 81B was extended from Hounslow like the 117. Most English place names have Anglo-Saxon roots, although their meaning can often be difficult to decipher. In the case of Hounslow the word derives from 'Hundes Hlaw', which means the barrow or burial site of a man nicknamed 'The Hound'. DGS22-2

David describes the location of this picture as Shepherds Bush. To be more exact I think it is Shepherds Bush Road with RTW10 heading towards Hammersmith on the 11. On a Sunday Riverside (R) garage's allocation on the route only went as far as the Aldwych. RTW10 entered service in 1949 along with the first 37 RTWs at Tottenham (AR) garage to work the 41 route. At that time the police would not give permission for 8 foot wide buses to operate in Central London. Before the war there would be no less than 80 LTs working the route. At this time in April 1961 there would have been 49 RTWs during the week. Dalston and Riverside shared the route, although at the weekend Victoria, Gillingham Street (GM) garage contributed about a dozen RTLs. RTWs operated the route from 1951 until early 1966. The 11 is one of London's oldest routes and it has remained relatively stable over almost a century. It's fascinating looking back at the clothing at that time. SGS22-3

This picture was taken the same day as the previous two in April 1961. RM284 is seen on the 220 in Shepherds Bush Road heading for Tooting station, where most journeys on the 220 terminated on Sundays. The 220 was a direct replacement for the 630 trolleybus route, which ran from Harlesden Craven Park to West Croydon vis Shepherds Bush, Hammersmith, Putney, Tooting and Mitcham. After the 630 converted, the overhead wires were left in situ for peak hour 655 service to Clapham Junction. However, this only lasted until November 1960 when Hanwell depot was converted in the stage 8 programme. The 220 has always been operated from Shepherds Bush (S) garage. RM284 arrived at S garage in November 1960 from Walthamstow. Two months before withdrawal in July 1992 it was reregistered to GVS447, and then scrapped later that year after 32 years in service in London. The vehicle behind is Dalston (D) garage's RTW274 on the 11. On a Sunday Dalston's allocation went through to the route's usual destination of Liverpool Street. DGS22-4

This is Wood Lane in the heart of the Becontree Housing Estate with RT3022 on route 87 passing through on its way to the War Memorial in Rainham. The scene is bathed in the late winter sunshine of early March 1961. The 87 was associated with Barking (BK) garage for no less than 68 years from 1934-2002. Prior to the RTs taking over in 1958, the route had been operated by RTLs since 1949 and before that by LTs. The RTs lasted 20 years on the route. The bus has come from Gidea Park, travelling in a roughly south westerly direction. Once it reaches Barking, though, it will completely change direction and head eastwards towards Rainham via Rippleside and Dagenham. DGS23-17

Upton Park (U) garage's RT2800 is pictured in Wood Lane on the 175 heading for Poplar, Blackwall Tunnel. During the week no less than four garages contributed vehicles to this route. Apart from Upton Park these were Barking, Romford North Street and Hornchurch. Unlike many of David's photos seen so far, this was not a Sunday since Upton Park had no allocation for the route on that day. At this time in 1961 the 175 could have potentially started out in Ongar, but journeys to Blackwall Tunnel would probably have started no further north than Chase Cross. Upton Park was unusual in housing both AEC vehicles (RTs) as well as Leyland ones (RTWs). The garage was situated very close to the former West Ham football ground. RT2800 spent four years at Upton Park, before moving on to St Albans (SA) garage in the country area after overhaul in 1963, during which time it acquired a green body. It was finally withdrawn in 1968. DGS23-19

David returned to Waltham cross in June 1961 to photograph the 649 which was due to convert the following month as part of the stage 11 programme. All the Edmonton routes had switched to diesel in April with the exception of the 649. This was because Stamford Hill (SF) depot had a small allocation on the route. Captured here is K3 1691. The conversion of the 649 marked the end of the K3 class. The replacing service for the 649 was the 149 and the route between Waltham Cross and Liverpool Street remained unaltered. As with most trolleybus conversions it was RMs that took over. Stamford Hill continued to have a small allocation after the changeover. The southern end of the route was strengthened by extending the 47 up from Shoreditch to Stoke Newington. On a Sunday you could now catch a bus from Stoke Newington all the way down to Farnborough in Kent, a journey that would have taken 90 minutes. DGS24-11

Another stable route has been the 137. For 53 years the service ran between Crystal Palace and the Archway, linking south and north London. Since the war the northern terminus has been Oxford Circus on Saturdays pm and on Sundays. So this is probably another Sunday photo. In 1961 the route would have been operated by RTLs from Gillingham Street, Victoria and by RTs from Norwood. Here we see one of Norwood's RTs, 4086, waiting at Crystal Palace to set off to Oxford Circus. Between 1964 and 2001 it was operated by RMs and RMLs. Today the route runs from Streatham Hill to Marble Arch and is run from Brixton (BN) garage using New Routemaster LTs. The 219m steel tower in the background was constructed in 1956 by BBC and is the main television transmitter for the London area. This bus stand was once where the Crystal Palace exhibition stood. It was built for the Great Exhibition of 1851 and originally stood in Hyde Park. After only a year there it was dismantled and re-erected on Penge Common and opened for a second time by queen Victoria in 1854. The Crystal Palace burnt down in November 1936. The fire was so big it could be seen from eight counties. Churchill described it as 'an end of an era.' DGS24-12

Three RTs wait at the former bus stand at Crystal Palace. The two routes seen here, the 3 and 63 are two more examples that remained stable over many years. The former operated between Crystal Palace and Camden Town from 1934 until 1987. At this time in June 1961 the route was shared between Norwood using RTs, as exemplified by RT3856 here, and Chalk Farm with RTLs. Then from 1964 until 1993 RM from Norwood and Chalk Farm garages ran the route. For a period Chalk Farm RML could be seen on the route at the weekend. Like many routes it has been shortened in recent years, first to Oxford Circus, then to Piccadilly and once more to Whitehall. In April 2023 it was diverted from Lambeth Bridge to Victoria via Horseferry Road and Victoria Street. The road in the background is the Parade, and beyond the wall on the other side of the road there is a sharp drop into a cutting along which the branch line from Nunhead to Crystal Palace (High Level) used to run. The line was run originally built by the London, Chatham & Dover Railway. Although it was electrified, it was closed in September 1954, two months after the line from Finsbury Park to Alexandra Palace closed. DGS24-14.

Passing through The Town in Enfield is Wood Green depot's K1 1277 on the 629, three days before the stage 10 trolleybus conversion was due to take place on 26th April 1961. In the background are three once familiar High Street names, Saxone for shoes, ABC which was a bakery and self-service tea room and a smaller version of Lyons Corner Houses, and Dunn & Co a gentleman's outfitters noted for their hat and tweeds. All had gone by 1990. The story goes that name Saxone derives from a shock football result when Kilmarnock beat Glasgow Rangers 6-1. As result a shoe company based in Kilmarnock changed its name 'Sax' being the scots pronunciation of 'six'. Later the pronunciation of the name changed to 'Sax-own'. I've always liked coming to Enfield to photograph buses. When I started recording the bus scene in 1973 this was one of the first places I came. One of the attractions of going there as a child was seeing green London transport buses. A bonus was a model railway shop on Church Street. DGS25-33

On the same day as the previous picture David has now travelled back to the other end of the route at Maple Street off Tottenham Court Road. It's amazing what a bit of spring sunshine can do to transform a scene. Here we see K2 1312 and behind it K1 1272, both from Wood Green depot. In a few days' time the route will become the new 269 operated by Routemasters from Wood Green and West Green garages. West Green had a small allocation of 5 RMs from Monday to Friday, but that only lasted until November 1961, barely six months. Wood Green alone then ran the route until it was withdrawn in 1968, when London Transport introduced its Wood Green W route scheme using single-deck Merlins MBs. The new W4 covered the Turnpike Lane to Enfield section and the 29 gained additional buses to strengthen the southern part. Whereas on M-F the route was scheduled for 39 vehicles, on Saturdays it was boosted to 46, I assume to cater for shoppers. DGS25-35

RT698 is passing through The Town in Enfield. Its destination is Durants Road in Ponders End, and that tells us that it's a Sunday working. Also the absence of people and vehicles hints at this. Until the early 1990s Sundays in Britain were very quiet. Very few shops were allowed to trade on that day. For the 107A Sunday was actually the main day in 1961 with 22 vehicles scheduled compared with just 8 on M-F. 16 came from Enfield and 6 from Edgware. All were RTs at this time. During the week the service ran through to the Royal Small Arms factory at Enfield Lock. RT698 entered service in June 1948. At that time it had a roofbox body. It possibly lost this during its overhaul at Aldenham in 1959. After overhaul it was sent to Enfield, where it stayed for the next 6 years. Almost its entire 21 year service in London was spent working from garages in East London. DGS25-37

RM114 is about to turn into Becontree Heath bus station on the 23. Prior to the November 1959 Stage 4 trolleybus conversion, the route had always been worked from Barking alone. Afterwards Poplar was given a small allocation of RMs to strengthen the route. Barking, though, continued to use RTs. RM114 was sent new to Poplar garage at the time of the replacement trolleybus programme, and it stayed at that garage for nearly ten years. Between 1937 and 1968 the route had run from Becontree Heath to Marylebone station. Then in 1968 it was cut back to Aldgate. Most of its 26 year history was spent in East London. After withdrawal it was sold to Clydeside Scottish in 1986. The school in background is Robert Clack Technical and dates from 1955. It became Robert Clack Comprehensive when it merged with a local Secondary Modern school in 1966. It is one of the biggest comprehensives in the country with well over 2000 pupils and a 16 form entry. Among its most notable students are the singer Sandie Shaw and the footballer Declan Rice, recently transferred from West Ham to Arsenal for a record fee of around £115,000. The man on the left with his suitcase could well be a rep of some sort. The car behind looks to be a Rover. DGS33-1

RT3605 stands in the yard at Romford, London Road (RE) garage. The 370s from Tilbury to Romford regularly turned there. David doesn't give the date of this photo, but I think it must be in early part of 1960 partly by the absence of leaves on the tree and partly by the fact that RT3605 went into overhaul at Aldenham in August of that year and was sent to Hatfield (HF) garage afterwards. I think the first car in the background is a four door post war Hillman Minx. Behind it is possibly a Ford Popular, which cost £390 when new in 1953. The steeple in the background belongs to St Andrews Church, built in 1862 for the new working class community there. A church in Anglo-Catholic tradition of the Church of England, it was built in the Early English style and is now grade II listed. London Road garage was opened by Edward Hillman's Saloon Coaches in 1932. It was taken over in 1933 by the London Passenger Transport Board (LPTB) and finally closed in 1977. It provided vehicles for the busy Green Line routes into Aldgate, the 721 from Brentwood and the 722 from Upminsteer Corbet's Tey, plus the 724 Romford to High Wycombe service. DGS33-14

RT4794 was part of the last batch RTs to enter service in February/March 1954. Like the previous picture this was taken in the yard at Romford London Road. In the background the houses are on Cotleigh Road, and there was an entrance to the garage on this road. The main entrance was on London Road. RT4794 was also the last one to be built with a Weymann body. It worked from Grays between 1959 and 1963. LPTB opened its Grays garage in 1936. The 370 was one of the main routes worked by the garage. It was stuated on the corner of Stifford and London Roads. Until 1951 Grays had been divided between LT and Eastern National for a number of years, but afterwards LT took over all the town routes and the area between Tilbury and Rainham. When London Country became privatised in 1986 it became London Country North East. After this there were a succession of changes with Arriva taking control. In 2008 Grays became part of Arriva Southern Counties grouping. This brought some stability, but since 2016 it has been part of Arriva London and now only runs red buses on the following routes;-66, 103, 248, 347,370 & 375. The old Grays garage closed in 1993 and relocated to Europa Park in West Thurrock. DGS33-14

When David took this picture in February 1960 at Stratford Broadway, RM188 had just entered service at West Ham garage. Apart from the 162 here it also worked on the 58, 69, and 272. The RM behind is on the 69 and the RT in the distance is on the 86. The 162 was introduced in February 1960 as a replacement for the two trolleybus routes 689 and 690, which were two circular routes from Stratford then around East Ham. The 162 was extended beyond Est Ham through to Barking, Longbridge Road, Goodmayes Road and up to Little Heath, replacing the 62 between Barking and Little Heath. The route was operated from West Ham by RMs and Barking had a small allocation of RTs from M-F. The church behind is St John's, built in the Early English style in 1833 and designed by the architect Edward Blore. The most notable feature is the three stage tower supported by flying buttresses. The clock, just visible, was designed by the famous clockmaker, Benjamin Vulliamy. It is now a Grade II listed building. Note the cobblestones. It's not difficult to guess what day of the week it is. DGS33-19

West Ham's K1 1101 is turning into Tramway Avenue heading for the Victoria and Albert docks on the 699. The route has about two months' left before the stage 6 trolleybus conversion programme will take place. This will see the end of the trolleybuses at West Ham. The 697 and its twin the 699 ran from Chingford Mount to Victoria and Albert Docks via Walthamstow, Leyton, Leytonstone, Stratford. Plaistow, at which point the two routes diverged before meeting up again at Connaught Road. At the end of April the two routes would be replaced by the 278, operated by RMs from West Ham. This picture gives a better view of St John's church and its clock. DGS33-21

M1 1540 stands in the yard at West Ham depot . From this angle it appears as if its trolley poles are not attached to the overhead wires. 1540 was one a small class of 25 vehicles designated M1, and based on the experimental 953. They were an AEC chassisless vehicle with bodies built at Weymann's factory in Addlestone, Surrey. They started entering service in November 1939. By early 1940 all were in service. For most of their careers they worked from the East London depots of Bow and Poplar. The latter's allocation went to West ham in 1953. The sensationalist Sunday newspaper, the News of the World, is advertising the serialisation of Alfred Hinds' story, for which they reputedly paid £30,000. Hinds was an alleged jewellery robber, who was given a 12 year prison sentence. He was nicknamed 'Houdini', for he escaped from maximum security prisons no less than three times. DGS 33-24

N2 1666 is the unidentified vehicle in the previous picture taken in the yard outside West Ham depot. Emerging from the shed it looks like it's about to set off to the Victoria and Albert Docks on the 687. The route ran from there up to Walthamstow, Crooked Billet via Freemasons Road, New Barn Street, Balaam street, Upton Lane, Forest Gate, Wanstead Flats, Leyton , Church Road, Markhouse Road and Blackhorse Road & Lane. The notice on the wall was the usual sign saying 'Trespassers will be prosecuted'. Whether it was in bus depots or railway sheds, I don't many of us took much notice of this such was our drive to get into these places. I don't think things really changed until privitisation in the late 80s and early 90s. Like the M1 the N1 and N2 classes spent most of their working lives on East London routes into Aldgate. The N2s were a small class of 24 vehicles. They had an AEC chassis and were the only class to have a Park Royal body. They entered service from June 1940 and lasted almost to the end of the trolleybus era in 1962. DGS33-25

Back at Stratford Broadway again and West Ham's L3 1435 is turning right out of West Ham Lane into the Broadway before heading north on the 699 to Chingford Mount. On the left is the former Swan Hotel. A pub with that name had been here since 1631. Later it became a coaching inn. It was rebuilt in 1921 and remained a pub and restaurant until 2005, after which it became a betting shop on the ground floor with flats above. The L3 sub-class first went into service from Highgate in December 1959 working on the hilly 611 route up to Highgate Village. The remainder went to Poplar and West ham for the Commercial Road routes. Totalling 150 originally the L3s were the first attempt in Britain at a large-scale production run of chassisless vehicles. Their arrival brought to an end the vast trolleybus expansion programme in London of the 1930s. DGS33-26

Heading along Greengate Street in West Ham, J2 981 from West Ham depot hasn't much further to go before it reaches its destination of Victoria and Albert Docks. On the destination blind, though, it just read 'Docks'. The trolleybus 699 route will shortly pass into history, its replacement being the new 278 route operated by Routemasters from the same West Ham garage. In the foreground on the right we can see part of a Victorian terrace. The houses the trolleybus has just past look more modern and substantial and may date from the Edwardian period at the start of the 20th century. Note the bay windows at the front on both floors. West Ham depot is on Greengate Street, but on the other side of the road. It opened as a tram depot in 1906. Trams gave way to trolleybuses in 1937 with the 699 replacing the 99 tram. Electric traction gave way to diesel in 1960. Finally in 1992 the garage closed to be replaced by one near Stratford. That in turn was replaced by a new and larger West Ham garage in 2008. DGS33-29

Stamford Hill depot's K1 1305 is seen passing Sam Levene's tobacconist and sweetshop heading north along Commercial Street. The area, known as Spitalfields, was once one of the poorest, the most overcrowded and crime-ridden in London. After the 1890s the area became settled by many Ashkenazi Jewish immigrants fleeing persecution in Central and Eastern Europe, many of whom worked in the rag trade. On Sundays the area comes alive with street markets such as Petticoat Lane. I remember it, though, as a rather depressing and dreary part of London. Hawksmoor's fine Christ Church used to be home to down-and-outs and meth drinkers. The bus will shortly be passing Spitalfields wholesale fruit and vegetable market. Since the market relocated in 1991 the northern part of the street has been undergoing gentrification, along with nearby Shoreditch and Hoxton. The southern part down towards Whitechapel High street is now very much a Bangladeshi area with excellent restaurants along Brick Lane. Jack the Ripper used to roam these streets in the late 19th century. Perhaps that's Mr Levene standing in the doorway of his shop. DGS34-2

Two of Stamford Hill (SF) depot's vehicles are off loading passengers by Shoreditch Church. The first trolleybus is K2 1229 working on the Sunday only route the 149A from Wood Green to Liverpool Street. Behind it is K1 1138 on the 647. It's blinded ready to return to Stamford Hill, so it will be finishing here and turning back via Curtain Road. The car moving away from the viewer is possibly a Morris Oxford 1000, while the one approaching is a Standard-Triumph 10, I think. The Watneys pub facing us on the corner of Hackney Road used to be called Horn(e)s. It later changed its name to Browns and still using that name it's now a lap dancing club. The pedestrians could well be heading for one of the nearby street markets. The nearest one to here is probably the Columbia Street Flower Market. The men are still dressed in Sunday suits and it would be rare to see a woman in trousers. This is summer 1961 shortly before the stage 11 of the trolleybus conversion in July affecting Stamford Hill and Edmonton depots. The 649A will become the new 243A and operated by RMs. 1229 is advertising the Hackney Gazette, the local paper still going strong. DGS34-4

Liverpool Street station was as far as either trams or trolleybuses were allowed to go along Bishopsgate. A once common sight, the young police constable with the white sleeve coverings is holding up the traffic to enable Edmonton's K2 1245 to make its turn. The 649 is blinded for Ponders End, which in practice would mean Enfield bus garage on Southbury Road. The bus behind is a 649A which will be heading back shortly to Wood Green Underground station. On a Sunday the streets around here were lined with stalls selling all manner of things, and it was always very crowded. The street opposite is Middlesex Street and just along there on the right is Petticoat Lane which gives its name to this market area. As the name implies, clothes were an important part of the market. I sometimes went there as a child with my Dad. What I remember most were the escapologists who would escape from sacks tied up with padlocked chains, sword and fire swallowers, and most colourful of all was the figure of Chief Monolulu, dressed in his African robes and feathered headdress. He would mingle among the crowds calling out, "Ah gotta 'orse!". Like Damon Runy0n's fictional character, Nicely Nicely Jones, he made his living selling horse tips. DGS34-6

A busy Victoria Coach station sees RFW3 preparing to a bay before taking visitors on a tour to Windsor and Hampton Court. Introduced in 1951, the RFWs were classified as AEC Regal Mark IVs, which meant they had basically the same chassis as the RFs. The 'W' stood for 'wide'. At 8 ft. wide they were 6 inches wider than the standard bus width. Like the Guy Specials (GSs) they had an Eastern Coach Works (Lowestoft) body. They designed solely for private hire work in and around London. In my last year at primary school we stayed at Sayers Croft Outdoor Learning Centre at Ewhurst in Surrey, and it was an RFW that took us there. Ewhurst was also the terminus of the 448 from Guildford and so I was able to see some of the GSs from Guildford while we were there. DGS35-36

Stamford Hill's K2 1326 is pictured at the London Docks terminus of the 647. The terminus was at the end of Dock Street, where it meets East Smithfield and The Highway. The address of the former Blue Anchor pub seen in the background, is given as No.1 The Highway, so The Highway must be the road leading away to the right. It looks like and was a grim, seedy run-area, for long steeped in poverty, and associated with cheap lodging houses, brothels, rough pubs and opium dens. One of my childhood memories is coming here, or at least nearby, and seeing above the roof tops a forest of ships' masts. Possibly they were ships moored in St Katherine's Dock. The scene today is almost unrecognisable to the one seen in this photo, such has been the regeneration of the area. Many years later I was to come back here while running the London Marathon. The replacement route for the 647 was the 67. It was extended via The Highway and Wapping Lane to terminate at Wapping station on the East London Line. DGS36-36

Edmonton's K2 1238 is turning at Enfield bus garage, which was referred to on the destination blind as Ponders End. In the background are three RTs on the 217 and 242. To the right of the picture Southbury Road climbs up to Southbury station. Here the road, which runs from Ponders End to Enfield town centre, crosses the recently reopened and electrified line between Lower Edmonton (now Edmonton Green) and Cheshunt (November 1960). The line had been mothballed since 1915. The station sits on the bridge. Along with Southbury, the stations at Turkey Street and Theobalds Grove were also reopened. DGS34-15

Driver and conductor relax beside their bus, RM766 at Aldgate bus station while working on the 253, the replacement route for the 653. When the route switched to diesel in February 1961 Highgate garage was given the sole responsibility for it, putting out 52 RMs M-F. This only lasted until April, and then Edmonton was given part of the allocation. However, their participation turned out to be short-lived and came to an end in the October of that year. Stamford Hill took over Edmonton's allocation. After that things settled down and there were no more changes until 1972 when Clapton (CT) garage took a share. Aldgate bus station, which is sometimes referred to as Minories bus station, was built in 1937 when the trams at Bow, Poplar and West Ham replaced their trams with trolleybuses. Unlike the trams, the trolleybuses needed space to turn. The new bus station was also used by buses and Green Line coaches. By 1947 it was the busiest bus station in London. DGS37-7

Stage 9 of the trolleybus conversion programme saw the final elimination of trolleybuses at Highgate depot in February 1961. The 239 was a like-for-like replacement for the 639, which ran from Moorgate, Finsbury Square to Hampstead Heath. In August 1961 Highgate's RM489 stands on the east side of Finsbury Square between duties. It looks like an office building has recently been demolished next to where the bus is standing. The 1960s saw the skyline of the City begin to change. From now on most of the new office building would be high-rise. DGS37-15

With three months to before the changeover at Finchley depot in November 1961 L3 1452 waits at the terminating stop on east side of Finsbury Square. The driver is spending a few moments reading the newspaper in his cab. The 609 normally went all the way up to Barnet Church, but if it was returning to the depot it would terminate at North Finchley instead. The depot was a short distance away off Ballards Lane on Woodberry Grove. After some of the Q1s were sold off to Spain, L3s were among those vehicles transferred in to Fulwell to replace them. One of them, L3 1521, had the distinction of being the very last trolleybus to run in service in London the following year. The vehicle behind looks to be RM373 and is working on the 271 route up to Highgate Village. Next to where the trolleybus is standing is now the recently built Liverpool University's London annexe. DGS37-16

Here is that very last trolleybus to run in service L3 1521. It is pictured here at the turning point at the top of Barnet Hill, blinded up for its next 609 journey back to Moorgate. I regularly used to take the 609 up to Whetstone from my school at the Angel, Islington to our school playing fields on Chandos Avenue. After stage 12 of the conversion programme, some of the Finchley trolleybuses were transferred to Fulwell and Isleworth to cover for the Q1s which went to Spain. Among them was 1521. On the final day of trolleybus operation it was working on the 604 Hampton Court to Wimbledon service. When it arrived back at Fulwell depot in the early hours of the 9th May 1962, it was greeted by a huge crowd of enthusiasts. Dad and I would often travel up to Barnet High Street to catch one of the buses to the Country area. We had the choice of the 303 to Hatfield and Hitchin, the 306 to Watford, the 342 to Hertford and the 84 to St Albans, the latter we could pick up at Arnos Grove. DGS60-6

Highgate depot had a small Sunday allocation of five buses on the 609, and this continued after Highgate switched to diesel. So for just over six months between late April and early November 1961, RMs from Highgate ran alongside Finchley's trolleybuses on the 609 on Sundays. This came to an end in that November when RMs came into Finchley to replace the trolleybuses there. Replacing the 609 was the 104, which to begin with covered the same route, Moorgate to Barnet. Highgate's RM582 has just passed High Barnet Underground station and will be climbing until it reaches its next and final stop on Barnet High Street. Among the other RMs noted working on the 609 were 580, 583, 585, 586, 588 and 589. The building on the left is part of Queen Elizabeth's Girls Grammar School. The bus behind is an RT on the 107A. DGS60-7

Merton (AL) garage's RT4379 has just crossed Hampton Court Bridge from the Surrey side, and continue on through Bushy Park, Teddington and Hanworth before reaching Feltham station. This rather circuitous route has started out from Mitcham, and despite all the changes the route has seen over the years it has always been linked to Mitcham. RT4379 came into service in 1953 and spent ten years of its sixteen year career in London at Merton and always remained based south of the Thames. For much of its 90 year history Merton garage has been associated with this route. The present Hampton Court Bridge dates from 1933 and is grade II listed. This is the fourth bridge on this site, the first being in 1753. The hotel on the right is the 4 star Mitre Hotel. It's also a restaurant, brasserie and wine bar. The car to the right of the bus is a Morris MO Oxford, designed by Sir Alex Issigonis, who later went on to design the Mini. DGS63-17

RT4592 is parked up at its home garage of Hounslow. To the right of the picture is the bus station. Hounslow has a very long association with the 81 route to Slough. Until 1963 it had a weekend extension with Windsor Castle, and for a couple of years between 1966 and 1968 it had an eastward extension through to Shepherds Bush on a Sunday. The bus behind is another of Hounslow's RTs 1139 on the 73, blinded up for the long journey back to Stoke Newington where I lived. Tottenham (AR) and Mortlake (M) garages were the mainstay of this route for the 73. Seeing RTs on the route at the weekend made a change from the usual RTLs, although when the LTs were replaced at both garages, Mortlake had RTs for a short period. Sandwiched in between the two buses is service vehicle 1122AS, an Austin LD van, which was used by the publicity department, and was based at Shepherds Bush garage. Where the bus station and garage are situated was once the short lived Hounslow Town station. It was built by the District Railway and was the terminus of a line from Acton Town. Originally the District had hoped to link it up with the London & South Western Hounslow station, which was why it built on an elevated level to bridge the High Street, but these plans were thwarted by the L&SWR, and so the District extended westwards to Hounslow Barracks (now West). The station was open between 1883 and 1886 and from 1905 to 1909. DGS63-31

The route number 400 was rarely used in London Transport Country Area days. The first time wasn't until 1958 when a Sundays only route from Addington (Park Way) to Warlingham Park Hospital was introduced. It began in June of that year and only ran 17 times before being withdrawn in October. Chelsham garage ran the route with a single GS. The second version, which appeared in 1959, was a Slough Town service running between Britwell Trading Estate (Wentworth Avenue) and Wexham Court Farm Estate, where it did a loop around the estate. Here we see Windsor (WR) garage's RT3219 standing adjacent to Slough railway station, out of sight on the right. RT3219 went into service in 1950 at Staines(ST) garage, moving to Windsor in 1954, where it spent eight years. The area on the other side of the road later became Slough bus station with the car park above it. DGS64-31

With ten days to go before stage 14 of the trolleybus conversion will see the end of trolleybuses in London, Fulwell's L3 1444 waits at the Vrow Walk terminus of the 604 at Hampton Court. On either side of the road horse chestnut trees are just coming into leaf. The car between the two buses is possibly a Vauxhall Velox with its hint of American styling. In the mid 1950s Vauxhall had a poor reputation for the build quality of its cars. Perhaps the two people walking towards the bus have just had a day out at Hampton Court Palace. The bus stop on the opposite side of the road is for the 716 Green Line service to Hitchin. DGS67-36

Hornchurch's RT1624 is on diversion off Heathway, Dagenham. It's heading along a side street on the Becontree Housing Estate in June 1962. The 175 will shortly reach on its destination at New Road, Dagenham, which indicates it was a Sunday. Also only Hornchurch vehicles operated the route on a Sunday. During the week three other garages were involved, Barking, Romford (North Street) and Upton Park. It was a complicated route with no less than 25 different route possibilities. Potentially the route could run from Ongar (Crispey Avenue) all the way to Poplar, Blackwall Tunnel. RT1624 is passing a boy on roller skates, who seems intent at looking at something in his hands. Note the well -trimmed hedges in front of the houses, nearly 40 years since they were first planted on the estate. DGS73-24

Another route in June 62 on diversion off part of Heathway was the 148 from Leytonstone to Dagenham. As this was a Sunday most of the journeys would terminate at New Road, Dagenham, but a few journeys went through to Fords at the end of Kent Avenue. Sometimes for these journeys the destination blind would just read 'Ford Works', omitting the 'Dagenham'. On Sundays the route was in the hands of Seven Kings (AP) garages RTs. RT2404 first went into service in November 1949 at Gillingham Street garage, Victoria, as part of a small batch to finish the conversion of the 52 to RT. Originally it had a Weymann body, but during overhaul in 1959 at Aldenham Works it received this Park Royal roofbox body. Personally I also preferred this type to the more standard one, perhaps because the first RTs I saw had this type of body. These would have been a batch of Mortlake RTs for the 73, which passed my home on Church Street. After overhaul RT2404 came to Seven Kings, where it was to spend its last four years in service in London. DGS73-26

Barking garage's RT1907 is turning out of Heathway into Hedgemans Road on its way on the 145 up to the Royal Forest Hotel at Chingford. This was a popular venue for North and East Londoners before mass ownership of cars, and particularly so at Bank Holiday times when there would be fairs there. There were fields where people could relax and have a Sunday picnic, and nearby there was Epping Forest for walking. The pub behind the bus on the corner of Heathway and Elm Church Lane dated back to 1839. Like many pubs all over the country it's no longer with us, having called 'time' for the last time in 2005. Double Diamond, the beer advertised across the front of the pub, was one of the best-selling beers until the 1970s. Originally it was known as Burton Pale Ale and dates back to 1822. It was heavily advertised by Ind Coupe on TV with the tagline-'A Double Diamond works wonders! On the other side of the road is a branch of John Collier, a men's tailor shop. Until 1953 it was known as the Fifty Shilling Tailors. Its tagline was 'John Collier-The window to watch!' DGS73-37

It is October 1962 and David went to Guildford to photograph there. GS21 is at Guildford's Onslow Street bus station working on the local 448A route to Pewley Way, a much sought after residential area high up on the edge of Guildford. Apart from the 448A Guildford's GSs worked on the 448 to Ewhurst and sometimes on the 436. GS21 first came into service at Hertford (HG) garage in November 1953. It arrived in Guildford in September 1961 and stayed there until 1964, after which it never stayed anywhere for more than a year and would go into store and then get relicensed. In November 1967 it turned up at High Wycombe to work the 442 serving the newly built Hicks Farm Rise estate. The GSs were my favourite vehicle, and desperate to see one, I persuaded my Dad to take me up to Hitchin on the 303 from Barnet, and there we saw GS2 on the 383 to Walsworth and Weston. DGS107-18

The scene in this picture is Upminster Road and RT3249 on the Green Line 722 route is passing RT4189 on the 370 at Upminster Bridge station. RT3249 was one of a batch of 36 green RTs which went to Romford, London Road garage in the summer of 1950 to run the two busy Green Line routes into Aldgate. This batch spent its 15 year career at this one garage and were never adorned with adverts. RT4189 is a Grays vehicle. Entering service in 1951 it was repainted red in 1968 and then spent 10 years in the Central Area. Upminster Bridge station was opened in December 1934 by the LMS railway, although its one island platform was only ever served by the District Line electric trains. The catenary belongs to the former London, Tilbury & Southend lines into Fenchurch Street which were electrified in 1961. The name of the station comes from a nearby crossing of the River Ingrebourne, whuch forms a boundary between Upminster and Hornchurch. The big advert on the bridge is for the local newspaper, the Romford Recorder. It is a chilly day in October 1963. DGS124-3

In his notes David writes that this picture was taken in Upminster. I'm guessing, but I think this might be Hall Lane by the absence of houses. The council estate at Upminster Park was well established by 1963 when this photo was taken, and this scene looks too rural. Perhaps the three ladies are on their way back to the estate from Upminster centre. Seven Kings garage's RT1694 has not long left Upminster Park Estate and is heading for London Road, Barking. This second version of the 193 was introduced in August 1959 as a trolleybus replacement for the 693. For quite a few years it was operated daily with RTs from Seven Kings garage. Barking also provided some vehicles for the route. Today the route runs from County Park Estate in Emerson Park to Queen's Hospital in Romford via Hornchurch, and is operated from Romford, North Street garage. The earlier version of the 193 was a short-lived affair running from Dagenham East to Dagenham Fords. It lasted just over a year from July 1957 until November 1958. DGS124-13

David G Savage

30th March 1944 to 7th August 2015